1001
Things to Spot
on the Farm

Gillian Doherty

Illustrated by Teri Gower

Designed by Susannah Owen
Edited by Kamini Khanduri

Isla,
There is
so much to see
on a farm.
When you
visit us we
will show you
as much as
we can!

Uncle Tom
Aunt Tracey
Katherine
&
Kirstin

2014

Series editor: Felicity Brooks
Series designer: Mary Cartwright
Agricultural educational consultant: Liza Dibble

Contents

Things to spot

The pictures in this book show different kinds of farms around the world. On every page there are lots of things for you to find and count. There are 1001 things to spot altogether. The example page below shows what you need to do.

There's a red balloon hidden in each big picture. Can you find them all?

Each little picture shows you what to look for in the big picture.

The blue number shows how many of that thing you need to find.

Milking time

3 milking jars   6 cows eating grass   7 goat kids   10 cow bells   2 cows sleeping

3 stools   1 calf feeding   7 milk churns   1 black bull   6 red buckets

There's a scarecrow puzzle on page 30.

There are all kinds of things to spot scattered throughout the book. You can find out what you need to do to find them all on pages 30 and 31.

The sheep farm

10 white sheep with black faces

3 dogs

1 shearing machine

8 lambs

10 poppies

4

9 rabbits

2 pairs of clippers

4 sheep with horns

3 shepherds' crooks

5 black sheep

The fruit farm

6 orange trees

9 birds flying

8 bags of lemons

2 donkeys

5 lemon trees

6

10 lizards

7 baskets of grapes

2 tractors

7 ladders

3 striped cats

The greenhouse

9 green tomatoes

2 forks

8 red strawberries

4 snails

10 cucumbers

10 red tomatoes

2 watering cans

5 caterpillars

7 empty plant pots

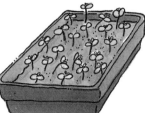
2 seed trays

Milking time

3 milking jars

6 cows eating grass

7 goat kids

10 cow bells

2 cows sleeping

3 stools

1 calf feeding

7 milk churns

1 black bull

6 red buckets

Baby animals

10 chicks

1 calf

7 lambs

5 puppies

2 foals

7 clean pink piglets

6 striped kittens

3 muddy piglets

4 black kittens

2 goat kids

Harvest time

1 combine harvester

10 seagulls

1 blue tractor

9 rabbits

10 bales of straw

1 baling machine 9 crows 2 grain trailers 3 red tractors 4 foxes

At the stables

7 saddles

6 bales of hay

5 sponges

2 foals

1 horse trailer

10 riding hats **3** black horses **7** forks **3** horse blankets **6** brown hens

The henhouse

1 fox

7 brown chicks

9 loose feathers

1 egg hatching

5 brown hens

8 mice   **10** yellow chicks   **2** bowls of grain   **10** brown eggs   **9** white hens

The rice fields

1 water pump

9 hats

3 kites

10 ducks

7 sacks of rice seeds

4 water buffaloes

8 baskets of rice plants

5 babies in slings

3 bicycles

5 black pigs

On the pond

10 ducklings   9 eggs   1 puppy   6 geese   3 birds' nests

22

5 ducks
swimming

2 duck
houses

7 goslings

6 dragonflies

8 fish

On the ranch

9 black cows

2 trucks

3 armadillos

9 cowboy hats

10 cows with horns

8 coils of rope 6 cowboys on horses 7 dogs 9 red bandanas 3 black horses

The honey farm

5 box-shaped beehives

4 smoke machines

5 bars of honey soap

9 pots of honey

3 pairs of white gloves

2 house-shaped beehives

3 white suits

7 dandelions

6 beeswax candles

1 pair of green boots

Tropical farm

2 sloths

5 toucans

10 cocoa pods

7 monkeys

8 sacks of coffee beans

4 yellow caps **5** baskets of pineapples **6** coffee bushes **3** snakes **4** bunches of bananas

This scarecrow is made from things found on the farms in this section. Look back and see if you can find which page each thing is from.

Sunflower

Carrot

Blue floppy hat

Pair of striped gloves

Long green coat

Yellow scarf

Spotted handkerchief

Spot 10 mice hiding in the scarecrow's clothes.

The answers are on page 32.

More things to spot

Did you spot any of these things?
Look back through the book to
see if you can find them all.

4 moles

8 blue butterflies

2 rakes

9 yellow butterflies

2 umbrellas

8 blue buckets

6 wheelbarrows

7 yellow buckets

6 brooms

3 squirrels

4 shovels

9 frogs

There are lots of people in this book. How many can you spot on each farm? Some of them are small or partly hidden, so you will need to search very carefully. The answers are on page 32.

The scarecrow

The sunflower is on page 7 (The fruit farm).
The carrot is on page 8 (The greenhouse).
The blue floppy hat is on page 13 (Baby animals).
The striped gloves are on page 27 (The honey farm).
The long green coat is on page 4 (The sheep farm).
The yellow scarf is on page 11 (Milking time).
The spotted handkerchief is on page 18 (The henhouse).

More things to spot

Did you manage to spot all the extra things scattered through the book?
Here's where they all were:

Moles
The sheep farm: 2
Milking time: 1
Harvest time: 1

Blue butterflies
The greenhouse: 1
The henhouse: 1
On the pond: 3
The honey farm: 3

Rakes
Milking time: 1
Baby animals: 1

Yellow butterflies
The greenhouse: 2
The henhouse: 2
On the pond: 2
The honey farm: 3

Umbrellas
The rice fields: 1

On the pond: 1

Blue buckets
Milking time: 2
Baby animals: 1
Harvest time: 1
The henhouse: 1
On the pond: 1
On the ranch: 2

Wheelbarrows
The fruit farm: 1
Baby animals: 1
At the stables: 2
On the ranch: 2

Yellow buckets
Milking time: 3
At the stables: 3
On the pond: 1

Brooms
The sheep farm: 1

Milking time: 2
At the stables: 2
On the ranch: 1

Squirrels
Milking time : 1
At the stables: 1
The honey farm: 1

Shovels
Baby animals: 1
Harvest time: 1
At the stables: 2

Frogs
The greenhouse: 1
Milking time: 1
Baby animals: 2
The henhouse: 1
The rice fields: 1
On the pond: 3

Did you count the people on each farm? Here's how many there were:

The sheep farm: 11
The fruit farm: 32
The greenhouse: 0
Milking time: 10
Baby animals: 0

Harvest time: 22
At the stables: 21
The henhouse: 0
The rice fields: 69

On the pond: 0
On the ranch: 18
The honey farm: 3
Tropical farm: 12

Acknowledgements

The publishers would like to thank the following individuals and organizations for providing information:

Fullwood Ltd,
Dairy Equipment Manufacturers,
Shropshire, UK

Frances Wood,
Curator of the Chinese Collections,
British Library,
London, UK

James Hamill,
Beekeeping Consultant,
The Hive Honey Shop,
London, UK

The Ranching Heritage Association,
Texas, USA